CELLS TO ORGAN SYSTEMS

JOSEPH MIDTHUN   SAMUEL HITI

BUILDING
BLOCKS

SCIENCE

WORLD
BOOK

www.worldbook.com

World Book, Inc.
180 North LaSalle Street
Suite 900
Chicago, Illinois 60601
USA

For information about other World Book publications,
visit our website at www.worldbook.com
or call 1-800-WORLDBK (967-5325).
For information about sales to schools and libraries,
call 1-800-975-3250 (United States),
or 1-800-837-5365 (Canada).

Building Blocks of Science:
  Cells to Organ Systems
ISBN: 978-0-7166-7860-1 (trade, hc.)
ISBN: 978-0-7166-7868-7 (pbk.)
ISBN: 978-0-7166-2951-1 (e-book, EPUB3)

Acknowledgments:
Created by Samuel Hiti and Joseph Midthun
Art by Samuel Hiti
Text by Joseph Midthun
Special thanks to Syril McNally

TABLE OF CONTENTS

There is a glossary on page 30. Terms defined in the glossary are in type **that looks like this** on their first appearance.

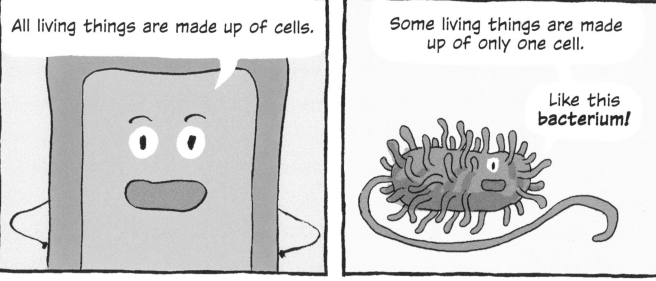

The human body has more than *10 trillion* cells!

Most cells are so tiny you can't see them without a microscope.

SEE?!

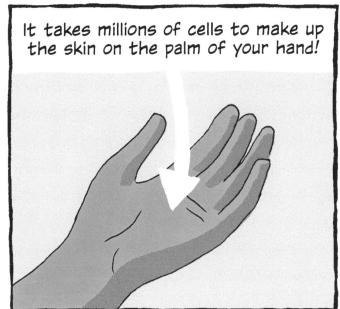

It takes millions of cells to make up the skin on the palm of your hand!

Just like you, a cell "breathes," takes in food, and gets rid of wastes.

Cells also grow and reproduce, or create their own kind.

And, just like other organisms...

...cells die!

GROWTH

Do you know one of the most amazing things about you?

At one time, you were a single cell.

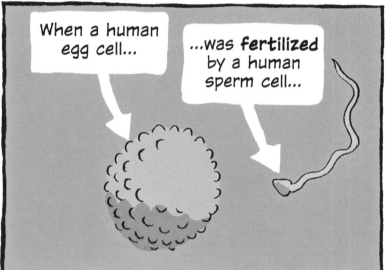

When a human egg cell...

...was **fertilized** by a human sperm cell...

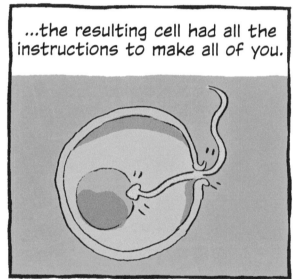

...the resulting cell had all the instructions to make all of you.

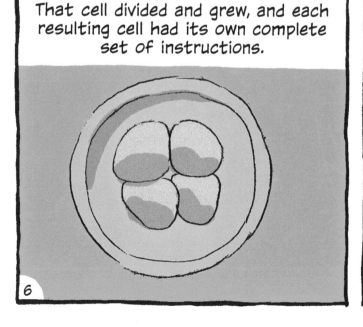

That cell divided and grew, and each resulting cell had its own complete set of instructions.

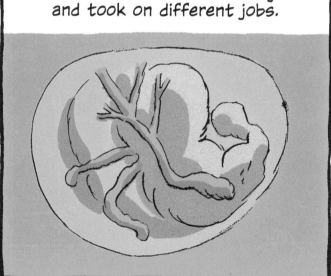

Over time, some cells changed and took on different jobs.

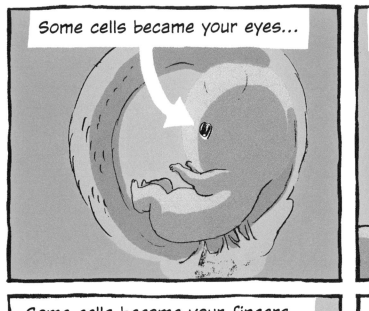

Some cells became your eyes...

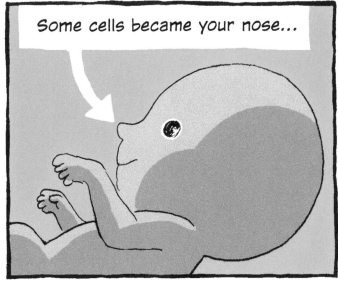

Some cells became your nose...

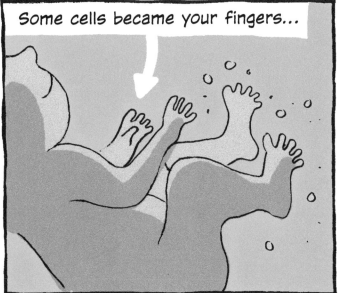

Some cells became your fingers...

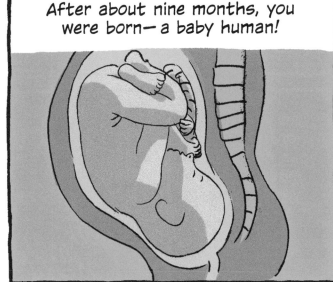

After about nine months, you were born—a baby human!

Your cells will continue to divide throughout your life.

That's how your body grows and repairs itself.

7

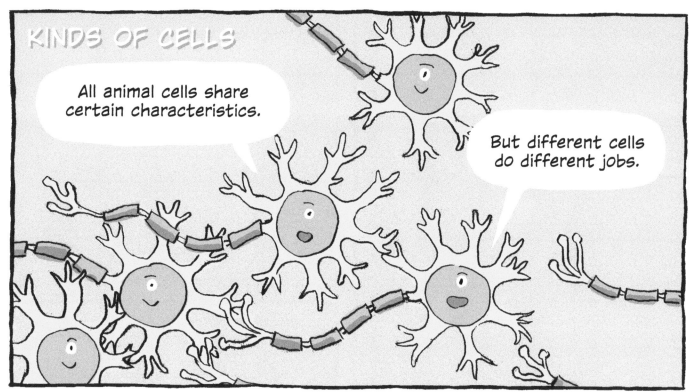

KINDS OF CELLS

All animal cells share certain characteristics.

But different cells do different jobs.

As you read these words, **nerve** cells in your eyes are carrying messages of what you are reading to your brain cells.

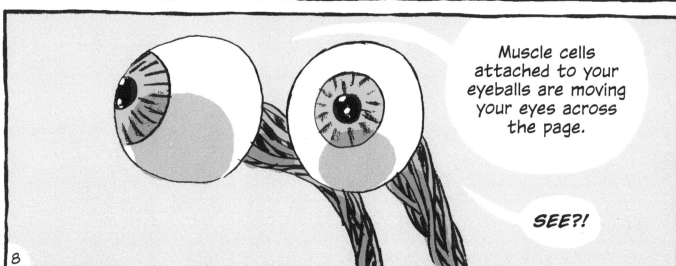

Muscle cells attached to your eyeballs are moving your eyes across the page.

SEE?!

8

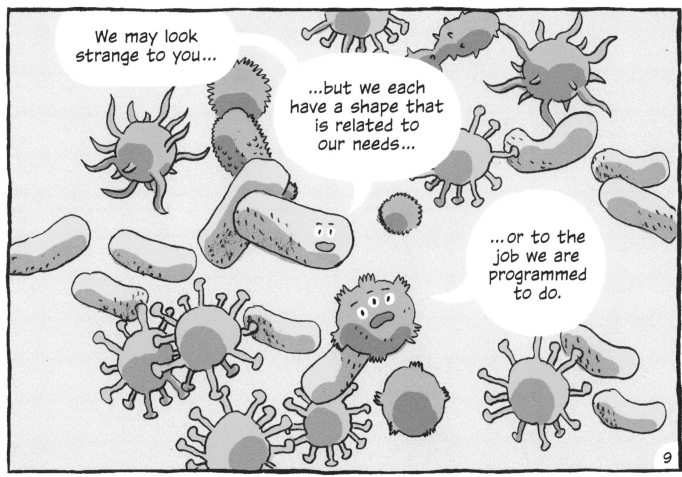

An animal cell acts like a tiny chemical factory.

It has a control center that tells the cell what to do.

It has power plants for generating the energy it needs to function.

And it has machinery for making its products or performing its services.

Beep
Beep

The **cell membrane** acts as a security system for the cell.

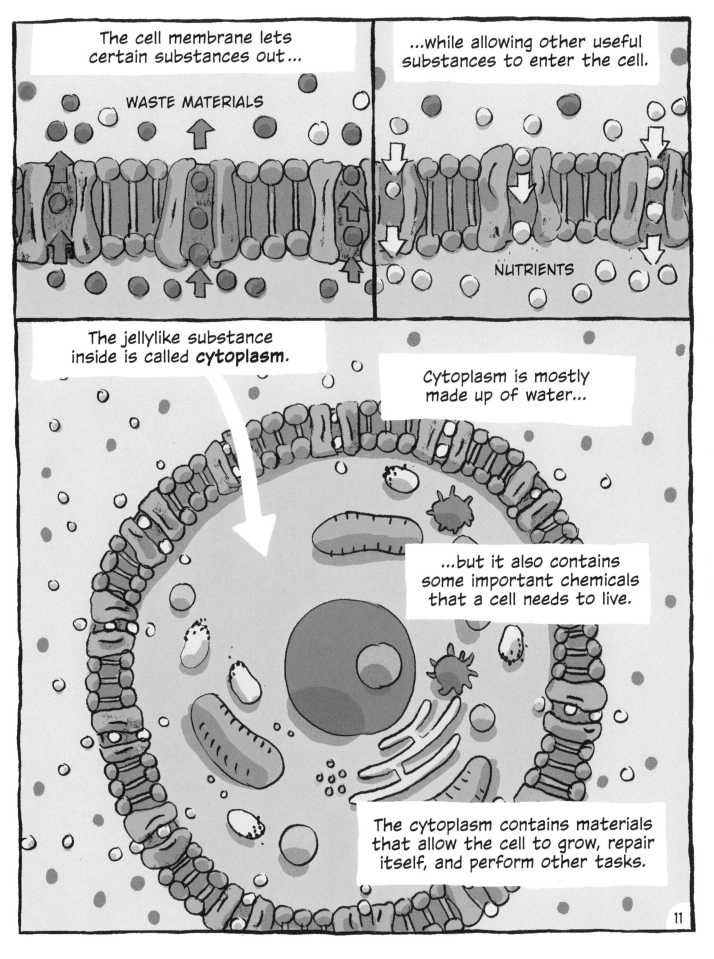

The cell membrane lets certain substances out...

WASTE MATERIALS

...while allowing other useful substances to enter the cell.

NUTRIENTS

The jellylike substance inside is called **cytoplasm**.

Cytoplasm is mostly made up of water...

...but it also contains some important chemicals that a cell needs to live.

The cytoplasm contains materials that allow the cell to grow, repair itself, and perform other tasks.

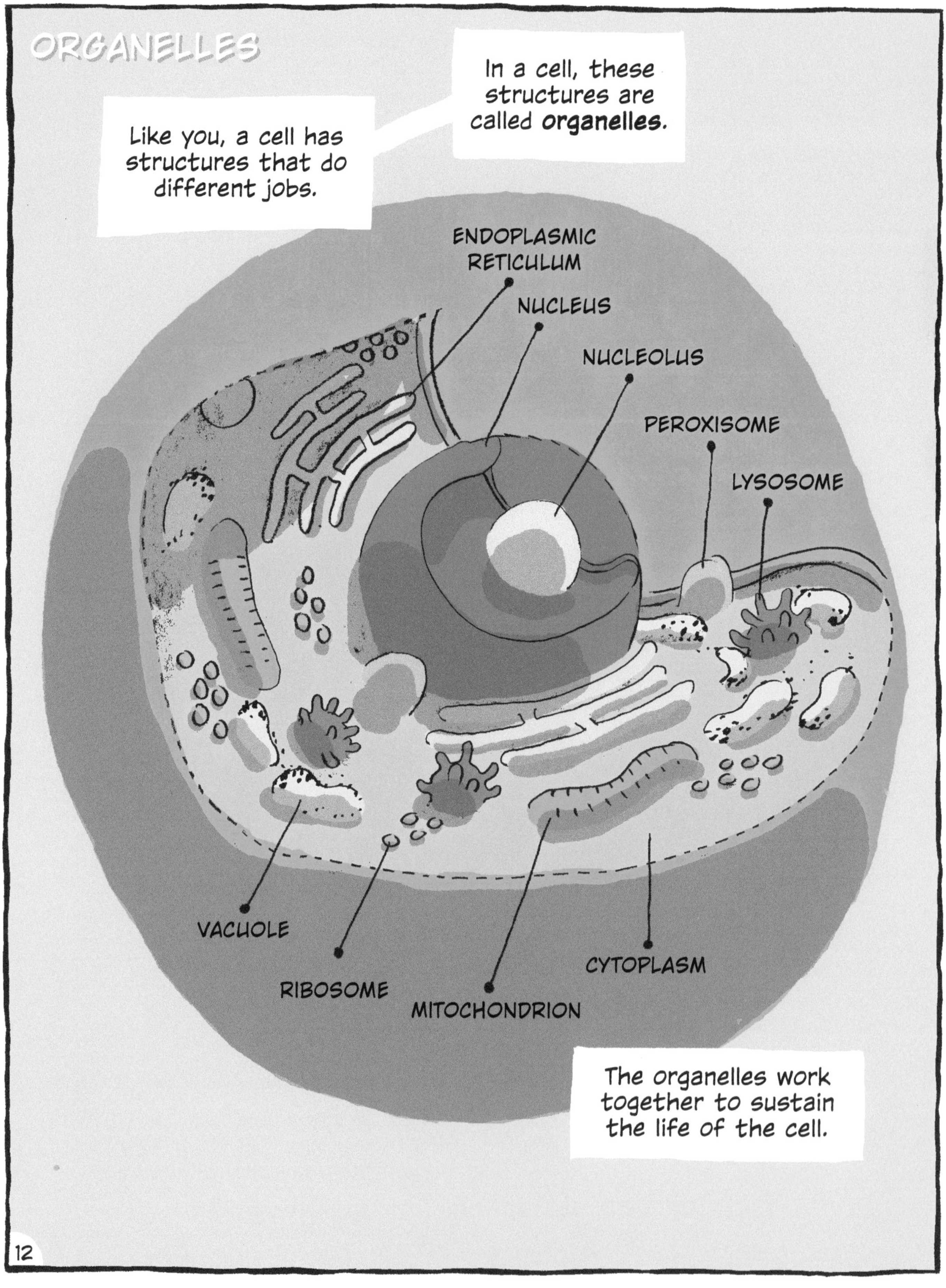
ORGANELLES
Like you, a cell has structures that do different jobs.
In a cell, these structures are called **organelles.**
ENDOPLASMIC RETICULUM
NUCLEUS
NUCLEOLUS
PEROXISOME
LYSOSOME
VACUOLE
RIBOSOME
MITOCHONDRION
CYTOPLASM
The organelles work together to sustain the life of the cell.

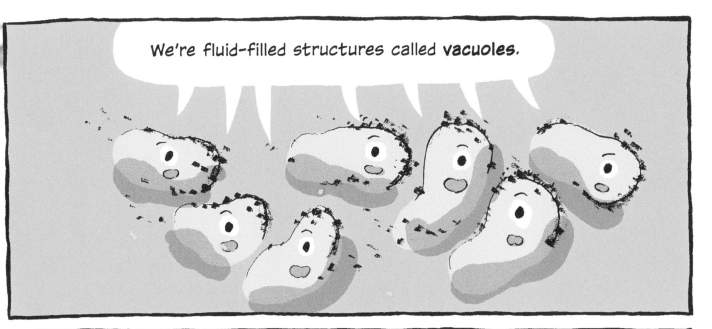

We're fluid-filled structures called **vacuoles**.

Vacuoles store the cell's food, water, and waste materials.

These materials can either be used by the cell...

...or removed if necessary.

When you eat, the food is digested inside your body.

Your body breaks down food into **nutrients** small enough to be used by your cells.

When nutrients enter a cell, they are "burned" as fuel by mitochondria.

This process provides your cells with all the energy they need to do work!

Your body uses this energy to send messages between nerve cells...

...contract a muscle...

...and turn the page!

NUCLEUS

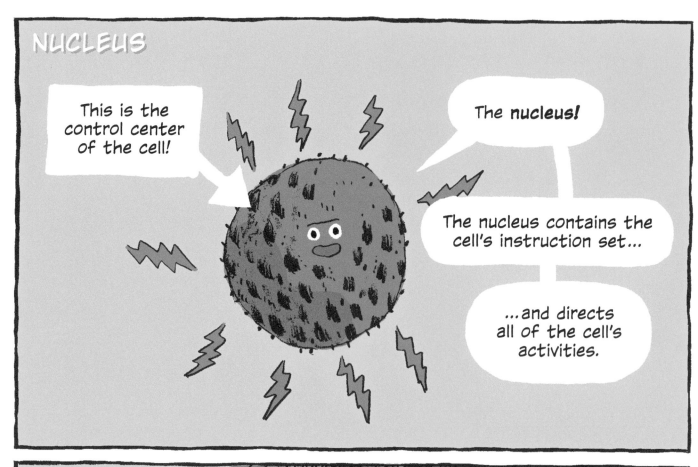

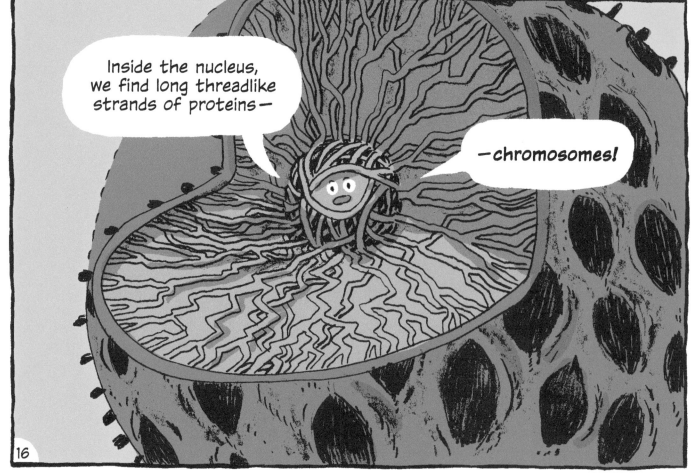

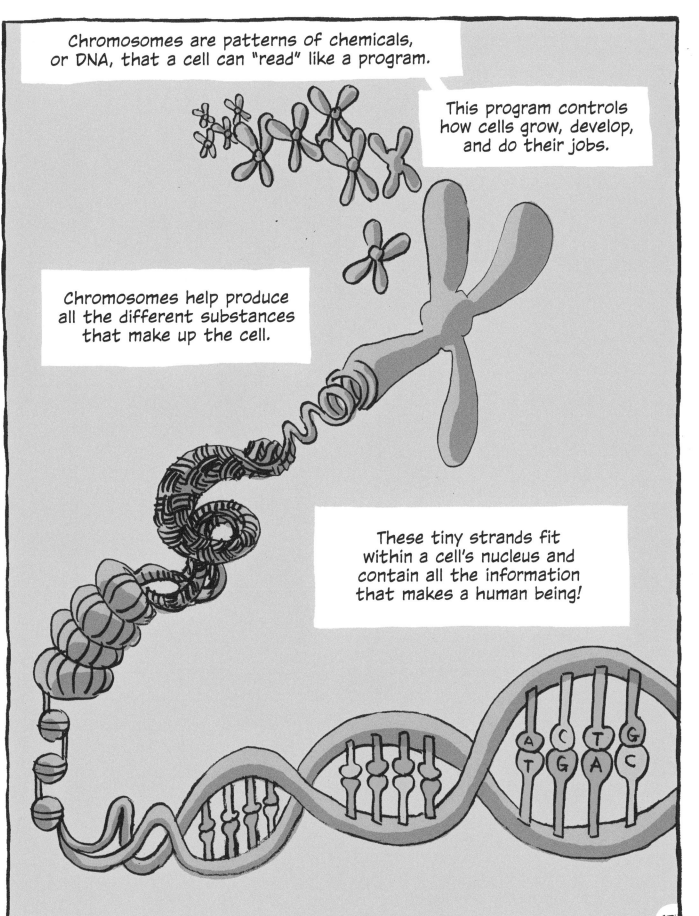

Chromosomes are patterns of chemicals, or DNA, that a cell can "read" like a program.

This program controls how cells grow, develop, and do their jobs.

Chromosomes help produce all the different substances that make up the cell.

These tiny strands fit within a cell's nucleus and contain all the information that makes a human being!

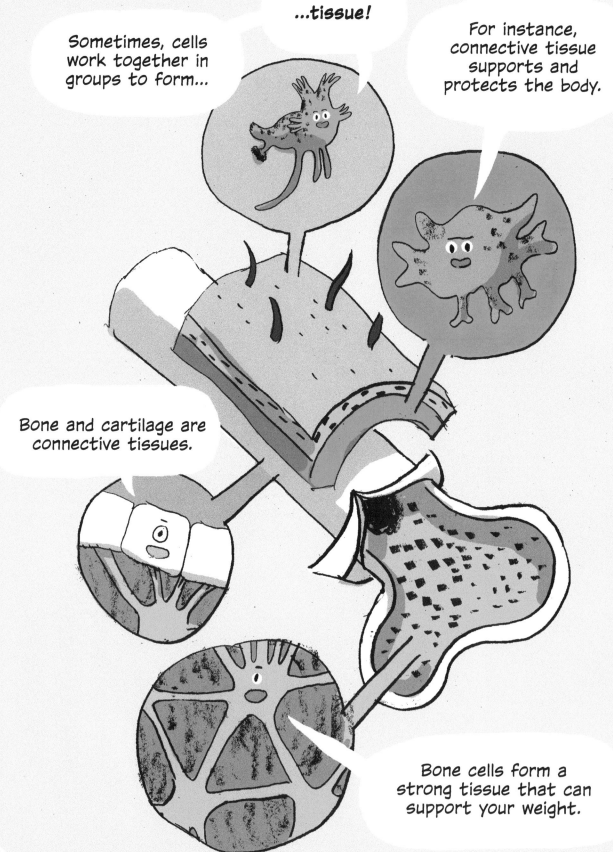

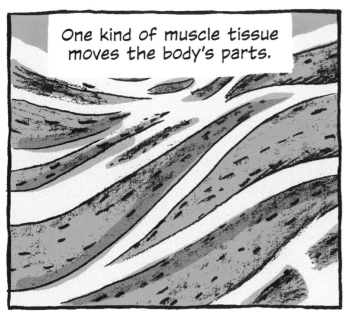

One kind of muscle tissue moves the body's parts.

Our job is to contract.

Those contractions are responsible for your wide range of body movements.

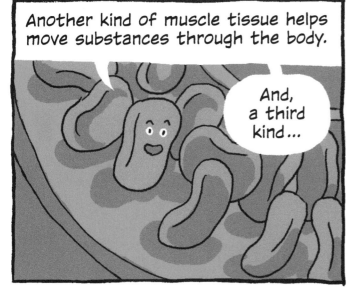

Another kind of muscle tissue helps move substances through the body.

And, a third kind...

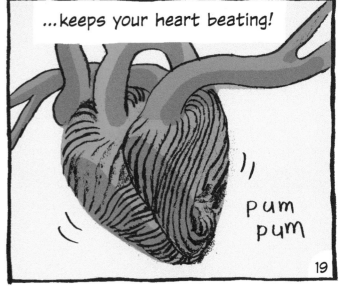

...keeps your heart beating!

pum pum

19

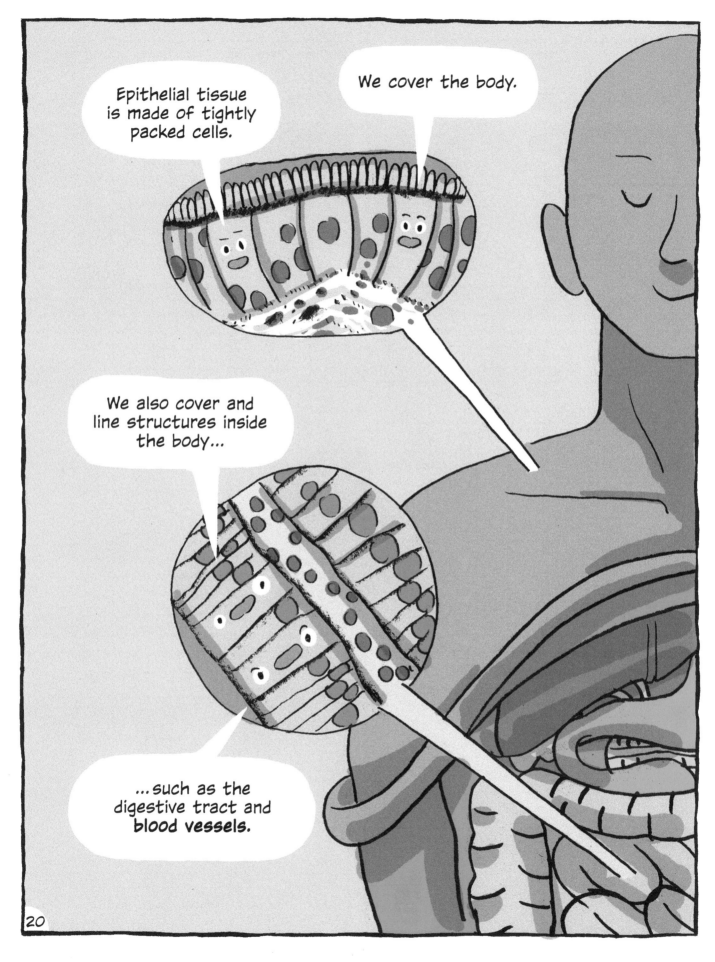

Nervous tissue sends signals that control parts of the body.

This tissue works to send messages from the brain...

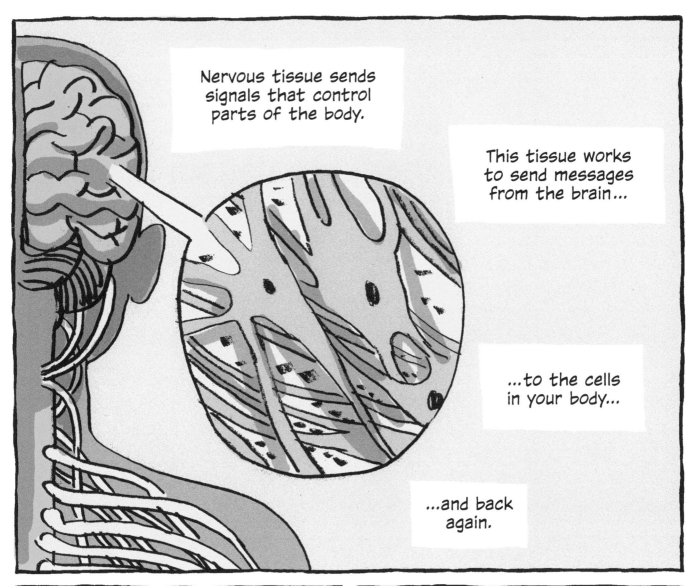

...to the cells in your body...

...and back again.

Nervous tissue allows you to coordinate many of your body's different functions...

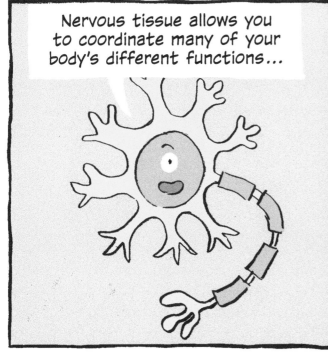

...and respond to a wide variety of stimuli.

KI-AI!

WIP

CRACK

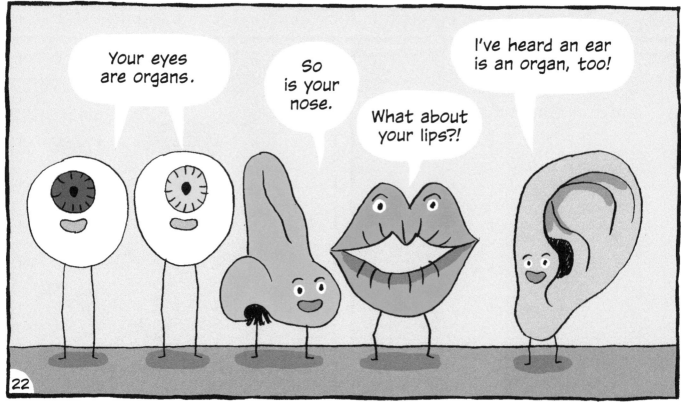

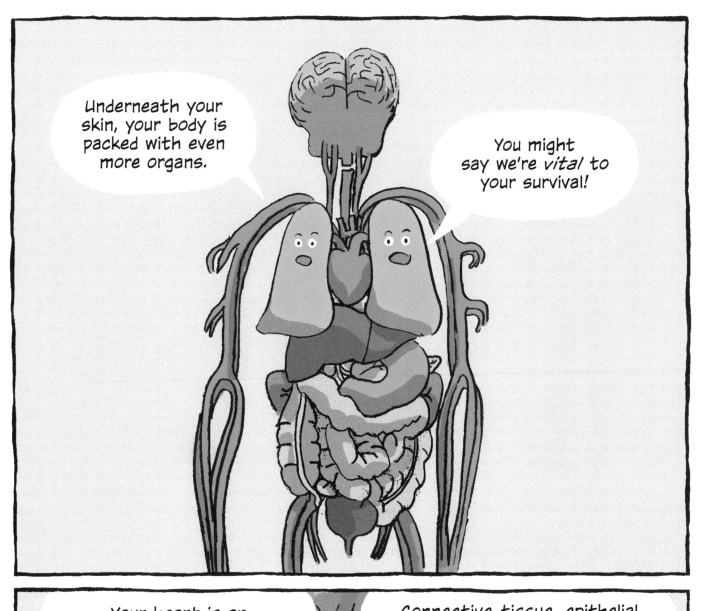

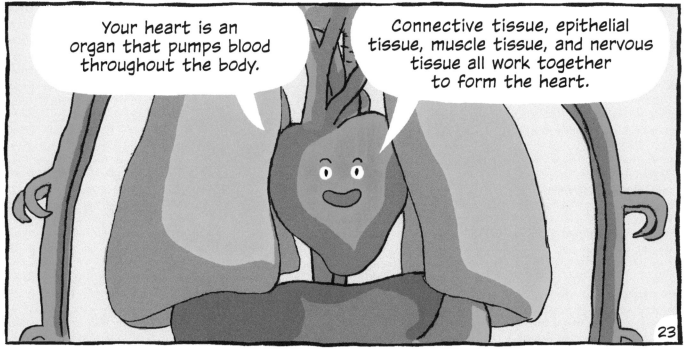

Just as organelles work together to form a cell...

...organs work together in groups to form **organ systems.**

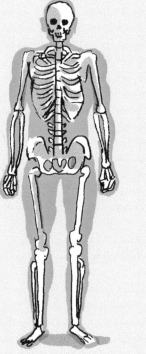

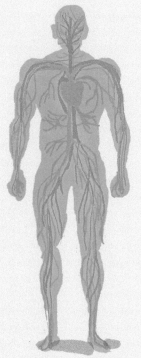

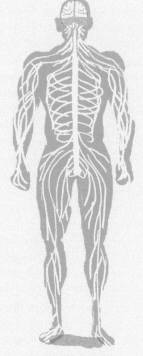

MUSCULAR

SKELETAL

CIRCULATORY

NERVOUS

Organ systems carry out major activities in the body.

RIGHT LUNG

LIVER

RIGHT KIDNEY

ASCENDING COLON

APPENDIX

SMALL INTESTINE

LEFT LUNG

AORTA

STOMACH

SPLEEN

LEFT KIDNEY

PANCREAS

DESCENDING COLON

BLADDER

URETHRA

The **digestive system** consists of organs that enable your body to use the food you eat.

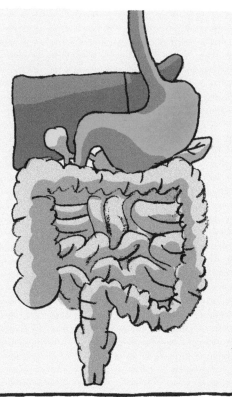

But, without the **urinary system** to remove waste, your body would become toxic, or poisonous.

Without your **respiratory system**, you wouldn't be able to bring **oxygen** into your body...

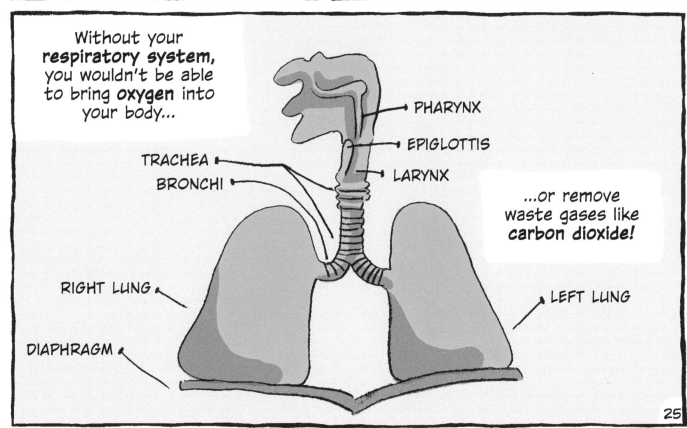

PHARYNX

EPIGLOTTIS

TRACHEA

LARYNX

BRONCHI

...or remove waste gases like **carbon dioxide!**

RIGHT LUNG

LEFT LUNG

DIAPHRAGM

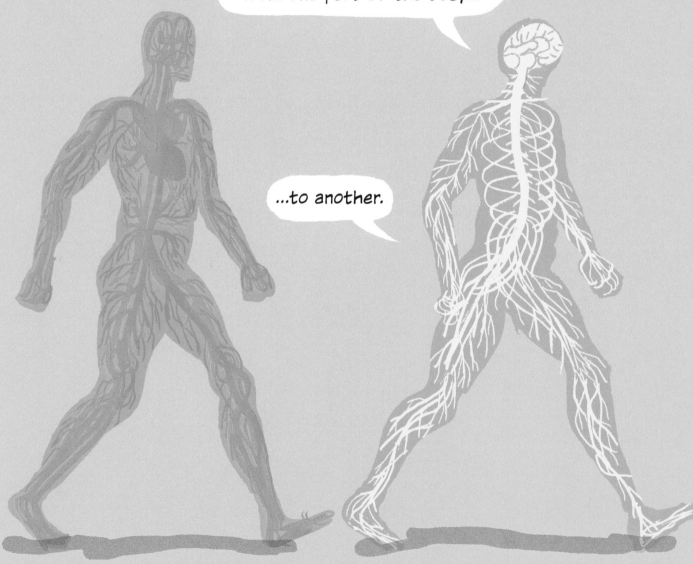

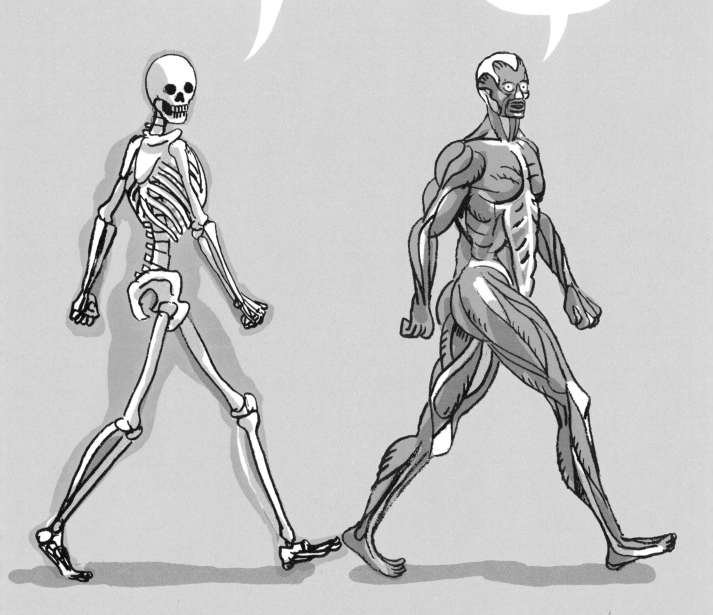

—or, should I say, we are?!

When you stop to think about it, you're quite an amazing organism—

Scientists are learning more and more about cells every day!

Some have even used their understanding of cells to grow human tissues and organs!

Others use computers to map the functions of cells in your body.

This helps us have a better understanding of why you are you.

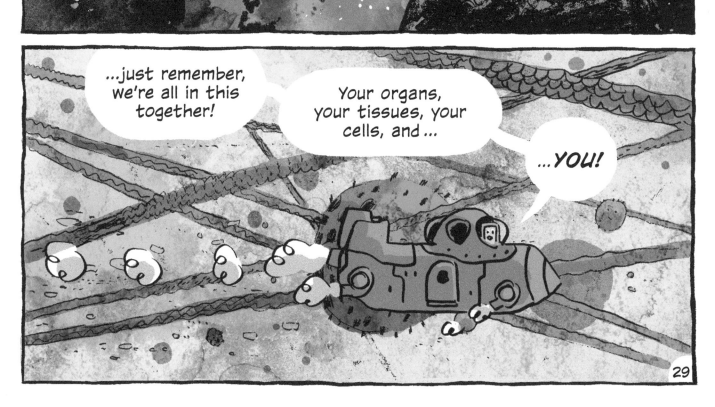

GLOSSARY

bacterium; bacteria a tiny single-celled organism; more than one bacterium.

blood vessel a hollow tube that carries blood and nutrients through the body.

carbon dioxide the air that is breathed out of the lungs.

cell the basic unit of all living things.

cell membrane a covering that separates the inside of a cell from the outside environment.

chromosome threadlike strands that direct cell activity.

circulatory system the group of organs that carries blood through the body.

cytoplasm the material that fills a cell.

digestive system the group of organs that breaks down and absorbs food in the body.

fertilize the process by which a male sperm cell and a female egg cell join together.

mitochondrion; mitochondria the "power plant" of a cell; more than one mitochondrion.

muscular system all of the muscles that cover the bones and move the body.

nerve a bundle of fibers that connects body parts and sends messages in the body.

nervous system the group of nerves and organs that controls all activities in the body.

nucleus the "control center" of a cell.

nutrient a food substance that helps body growth.

organ two or more tissues that work together to do a certain job.

organ system two or more organs that do a common task.

organelle an organlike structure within the cell that has a specific job.

oxygen an essential gas that is breathed into the lungs.

respiratory system the group of organs that brings oxygen into the body and removes carbon dioxide.

skeletal system the entire collection of bones and tissues in the body.

tissue a group of similar cells that do a certain job.

urinary system the group of organs that removes wastes from the blood.

vacuole a small storage space in a cell.

FIND OUT MORE

Books

Cells, Tissues, and Organs
by Donna Latham
(Raintree, 2009)

Hear Your Heart
by Paul Showers
(HarperCollins, 2000)

Human Body
by Richard Walker
(DK Children, 2009)

Human Body Factory: The Nuts and Bolts of Your Insides
by Dan Green
(Kingfisher, 2012)

Repairing and Replacing Organs
by Andrew Solway
(Heinemann, 2008)

The Way We Work
by David Macaulay
(Houghton Mifflin/Walter Lorraine Books, 2008)

Tissues, Organs, and Systems
by Karen Bledsoe
(Perfection Learning, 2007)

Ultra-Organized Cell Systems
by Rebecca L. Johnson
(Lerner Classroom, 2007)

Websites

Biology 4 Kids: Cell Structure
http://www.biology4kids.com/files/cell_main.html
Get an in-depth education on all of the parts that make up a cell.

Kids Biology: Biology of Cells, Tissues, Organs, Organ Systems, and Organisms
http://www.kidsbiology.com/biology_basics/cells_tissues_organs/structure_of_living_things1.php
Learn all about the cells, tissues, and organs that make up your body systems by watching short videos and reading fun, fact-filled articles.

Kids Health: How the Body Works
http://kidshealth.org/kid/htbw/
Select a body part to watch a video, play a word find, or read an article to learn more about its function in the human body.

Kids Konnect: The Human Body
http://www.kidskonnect.com/subjectindex/31-educational/health/337-human-body.html
Tickle your brain with some fascinating fast facts about the body's many systems.

Kids.Net.Au: Biological Cell
http://encyclopedia.kids.net.au/page/bi/Biological_cell
All of your questions about your body's cells will be answered in this detailed article.

NeoK12: Cell Structures
http://www.neok12.com/Cell-Structures.htm
Watch videos that illustrate the structure of cells, and then take grade-specific quizzes to test your knowledge.

Science Kids: Human Body for Kids
http://www.sciencekids.co.nz/humanbody.html
Sample a range of educational games, challenging experiments, and mind-bending quizzes, all while learning about human body topics.

INDEX

CPSIA information can be obtained
at www.ICGtesting.com
Printed in the USA
LVHW07*1603130318
569700LV00025B/410/P